For Philippa, at Launde,
April 2001

with best wishes

Running with the Unicorns

Joanna Boulter

The Bay Press

First published 1994 by: The Bay Press
7, Collingwood Terrace
Whitley Bay, Tyne & Wear
NE26 2NP
Tel: (091) 252 6186

Typeset by David Stephenson
at Isis Arts, Wallsend
in Palatino

Printed by Peterson Printers
South Shields

ISBN 1 899462 01 5

Thanks are due to the editors of Orbis, Writing Women, Iron Press and Vane Women Press, who first published several of these poems.

The Bay Press acknowledges the financial assistance of Northern Arts.

In memory of my mother

Contents

The Courtship Dance of Cranes

The bed looms huge in the room's
dimness. Squat dark mahogany oppresses,
velvet drapes stifle the air. The door
closes inexorably behind her.
Opposite, a screen, firelight fluid
on gold, delineating almost with life
the stark black and white of the birds.

Her heart beats against the cage of her ribs,
shaking her: the cranes move
delicately across their gilded ground.

They dance, gravely formal, according to
the pattern of instinct. Watching, she broods
upon the shape of this day: the display
of white silk and rosebuds, of dark frock-coat;
the solemn symmetry of processions,
receiving-lines; this unknown pas de deux
that he and she now find themselves performing.

The cranes circle each other, treading
with poised elegance their part
in the year's pattern, which instructs them.

And she is aware now of herself as dancing
one tiny sequence in the corner of
a great design. Steadily, she unhooks
her bodice, unties the ruched plumes
of her crinoline. Petticoats sigh to the floor.
Slowly she extends one after the other
her slender legs, slips off the ruffled drawers.

On the other side of the screen
the cranes attend her. Feathers tremble.
They elongate their necks.

Soon, he will enter the room,
will iterate her movements according to
the screen's patterning, sleek black,
flounced white finery lying at last
side by side. The birds entwine their necks.
Blood thrums in her throat. A changed life
stoops, flutters, hovers over her.

The Nightingale in Love

(*Le Rossignol en Amour* - after Couperin)

"I'll play this one
for you," you said, out of the blue.

No prelude, then; simply, a private hearing
at a public concert. The sopranino,
smallest of the recorder family,
warmed in your breast-pocket while I sat
anonymous in the hall, schooling my face
to purely musical response.

I watched you lip the pipe
before me, breathe life into it,
tonguing the phrases into flowing shape
as underneath your hands the music grew.

Oh, the roulades, the liquid melismatic
tremblings of sound, the fainting ecstasies,
bravura passions! mellifluous risings and fallings!

The craft of it! Seduced by a vibrant column of air!

And dared I trust
such practised trillings, as bird, composer, player
poured out his heart with that consummate skill?
I thought I heard
the plangent note of genuine artistry;

but only know, every performance since
borrows your breath, your lips, to tell again
those passionate promises.

Flag Fen

Gods of willow and alder
whose roots sup the fen
whose boles are our bulwark
against shifting ooze
whose branches stay us
safe upon silt
whose boughs shield us
whose bark heals

Guardians of the Causeway
I set your tokens
beneath the weft of our lives
under our lodges

in blessing and in beseeching

that the fens feed us
that the mere not weep salt tears
that floods not engulf us
that agues not shake us
that all our foes be land-bound!

*

Heron at reeds' edge
stock-still amid sedge

dawn-dim and dusk-dim
both alike to him

bright unblinking eyes
glinting with knowingness

watching rich eddies
conning likely places

there where eels coil
he stabs with his bill

alone he feeds
apart from all his tribe

and alone I wait
the clearing of my Sight

*

The night of the raft-people
when the eel-men came
blue squirled between their eyes
I felt their ripples in my soul
we were not unready

dark watching till sword-clash
we took them as we take
the fanged pike in wicker baskets
we tossed their bones to the mud
their blood we spilt to the water

I gave a son that day
to the mere's mothering.

Nor I only.

*

Between womb-waters and life-spring
the birth-blood clots. We dip our newborn children
so that the fen will know them.
Naming and cleansing are one.
And at the ebb
after the thick blood's stoppage
we give them back to the waters.

Our lives flow first between sedges
then broaden into the wide mere
open and shining with light.

Dark still lurks at the edges
but we build our lives
we fish and hunt
raise crops and livestock
where the light is bright.

The mere is our mother.
Children play at her breast.
She feeds and guards us
and carries us in her known arms
through the last dread darkness
down to those great waters
beyond living sight.

*

This hallowed child
at his first dipping
the waters held his breath.

His mother weeps
knowing him too good
for womanly breast.

Little friend
we give you back whence you came.
Beseech your Mother for us

for healing of sorrow.

Clifftop Burials at Whitby

After the heavy air of the deathbed,
hours crouching close to catch the last words,
suddenly the wind clenches them like a fist
there on the clifftop. It would snatch
the very coffin if they relaxed an instant.
There is no shelter from walls or draperies.
Black cloaks flap like bats, veils are convulsed;
above jet mourning brooches the wind chisels
a tear-channel down the stoniest of faces,
and voices naming the departed yet again
are thinned by it to palimpsest.

Mortality might perhaps have been enough
to battle at, without this unseen foe
that, bodiless itself, takes and distorts
all that it clutches. But they
have struggled up into its territory,
a trespass seeming beyond all reason,
painfully wresting from air this one
particular plot. An act of defiance, maybe,
against corruption, an attempt to court
eternity, preserved ancient as ammonites
in that rocky soil. Or perhaps an act of faith,
those bitter laborious valedictions
already halfway to heaven. Perhaps.

But the wind, sharpening its teeth on stone,
gnaws at the faces of memorial slab
and box tomb. It feeds on the names
greedy as a cancer, it ulcerates
in memoriams past hope of recovery.
And as the stones crumble, the named selves
lick thin and vanish, consumed into the air.

Ancestral Voices

In this cold country
they make bones dwell in boxes. As for the wood,
its trees were strangers to us.

We shiver naked in an alien dark
till they expose us to the shock of light
cruel as caged lightning, to dead air.

They deal with us briskly. If I were a stone
I would not care to be handled so.

They measure us
with profane fingers, they talk across our heads.
Then put us back into their dark. We do not know
where we are, only where we are not.

Our bones ache for the soil our ravaged flesh
already enriches. Our spirits cry
to the land of the red rock.

Children, fetch us home.
Bury us where these cold men dare not come.

Tool-Maker

The flint flakes
clear-cracked, edge nudged
sharp and sheer. Run your thumb
gently along its fang; the blood springs.
Your blood for the stone's power, to give you life.

Itself will cut Itself,
splinter the dark bone of stone
only on one of its own kind.
Find, cruel, the split in its spirit
and strike, fearless, to hone its cruelty.

You cannot kill it.
This stone is numinous with life.
It has more life than the deer
it shears and shares, spares not sinew and skin.
It has more life than the branch
it hacks, the stalk, the leaf it cleaves.

It is more hard with life than anything on this earth.

Before I strike I speak:
Heart of flint, forgive me for what I must do.

The Collaborator

When the old dog barked, I went out with the lamp
into the wet yard, not knowing what I'd find.
A fox, perhaps, or a few Allied soldiers
looking for billets. The enemy, they said,
were in retreat, away across the Loire.
And then I saw the grey
of his tattered uniform, and my heart clutched in fear.

But it was only a boy, rain-soaked and wounded,
bewildered by a war nobody understood.
I had to cut away
the matted blood that darkened his hair.
When he spoke his voice caught
on that uncouth speech, from youth, tiredness,
those gutturals maybe. I don't know what
he said. I think he was trying not to cry.
I looked away
and poured him milk. I never had a child.

When the dog barked again, he was the one
who started. I put my hand on his,
and so they found us, sitting at the table.
And took him. He looked at me,
and from somewhere summoned up this incredible smile
for the enemy who reminded him of his mother.
I remember it to this day

as I remember the rough hands, the cold razor
over my scalp, the jeering; but no shame,
no shame at all. I would do it again.

The Taxidermist's Tale

Late again. He heard her key fumble, heels clack,
nosed her perfume through the halitus of the workshop.
She said it clung. Always used too much scent.
Now he gagged at the reek she brought in

of stale smoke, flat beer, sour sweat. Life,
she called it. The beat of dance-music still glazed
her eyes, rimmed with black stuff; her dress clung,
exposing her shape. He felt defiled, to think

of those other eyes licking at her. So,
smiling, he embraced her. Rigid, the point
slid voluptuously between the bones of her neck.
She quivered and was still. He withdrew;

wiped the blade clean. Then gently bathed away
the cloying vanilla smell of her face-powder,
a smear of plum-juice from her lips, that fly-trap
of spun sugar out of her hair.

Cleansed, she was his again. Should he forgive?
His heart thudded like a drumbeat, but his hand
was steady as ever. The scalpel drew
its first fine line down her whiteness.

Tenderly he began to disrobe her. Now at last
his skill was potent to keep her at his side.
Her remorse could not move him, no matter how
the red skull wept. He was pitiless.

Her skin clung to him; he put it aside.
Sharp as a knife his need drove him
through to her core. Never since Adam's rib
had man and woman known such intimacy.

His hands sleeked her bones, polished them
with breath, spittle, semen. Naked
he triumphed in her utter nudity. Then rose,
began to reconstruct their lives.

He wired joints, forbidding dancing. Over the frame
he shaped padding to his own hands. He cupped
her breast, her haunch, privately. Closer than those dresses,
and all for him. He had made supple her skin

with borax. Formaldehyde would have served
her right, the things she'd said about the smell;
but that was for heavier hides. He eased her back
into her covering, smoothing up from extremities

as though dressing her in silk stockings. His thread
was fine as a hair, needle his slenderest curve.
As for his art, that surpassed itself. And she
was wholly his at last. He sat and smiled

at her. She gazed back. The glassy stare
reminded him of that night. There were other girls.
Prodigious skill twitched in his hands. He craved
to feel again that bone-deep consummation.

Whip Hand

The spotlights lend
a spurious gloss to their coats. By day
two have a touch of mange, the third
worries despondently at
a cankered ear. Nothing serious.
They'll see the vet when there's time. Meanwhile
they slink every night into the ring
along their fenced entry, into their own personal,
safe, arena. He invades this. Every night
he's in there with his whip. They drag their bellies
along cow-smelling turf, reluctantly make
that cramped spring to the barrel-halves.
He rarely needs to touch them. Their tails twitch,
tentatively, lips lift in the travesty
of a growl. The public like it when they snarl.
It keeps their illusions alive.

Buttoned to the neck, his wife
sits in the caravan, her own private space,
doilied and figurined, that he will be permitted
to enter, scrubbed clean
of the fusty, acrid smell of indoor lions.
She knits, listening to the distant applause,
the muffled roars. Her lips twitch
in a caricature of a smile. She likes it
when they snarl. It keeps his illusions alive.

The Princess of the Parabolas

She'd seen him this afternoon behind the stables
with the bareback rider, that vapid posing blonde
that leads the parade, gelding between her thighs.
Now her feet on the ladder tread down
that memory, pushing it further and further
beneath her as she mounts. Her eye reminds
her solely of the learned distances,
the unmarked boundaries of the realm of safety.

Everything waits. The ring below round as a mouth
gasping; up here the dome of breathed-out air
the two of them must decorate. She traces
curves in her mind, locks them onto the void.

He smiles at her in his scarlet leotard,
grasps the bar with his ankles. His hands entice.
She knows the failures of trust, the rotted net,
the careless knot: these are the tales
of their profession, as much as the great feats.

In this blank space there is no room
for hesitancy. She palms starch, shapes herself
for the aerial geometry. Bright teardrop
spangles glitter, too fast for the eye to catch.
Forget that prissy piece! Could *she* do *this*?

Terminus

Dream after dream I've searched for you, knocking
on strange doors, in towns never visited
whilst waking - but always near railway lines -

and sometimes getting the right house only to find
you not at home, so that I have to face
your family's polite bewilderment.

Last time, you came to me. You wished, you said,
to satisfy yourself that I was well
and happy. There was no embrace. I leaned

my face against your shoulder's warmth and felt
remembered comfort; saw you to your train;
waved you away; and woke to feel afresh

the grief of our remembered parting stab
with sudden sharp perception of your death,
and the continued grief of no more dreams.

Maiden Castle

After so steep a climb
I could not beat back one man
(as it might be, you)
leave alone a defending tribe.
Merely to oppose this hill
is strife enough and more.
But those in the ancient past,
Celt against Celt who came
for plunder or revenge,
could creep up almost at leisure,
the woods came up so far;
and in that tangle of trees
their eyes still watch and wait
as they catch breath, bivouacked
behind blackthorn and hazel,
and choose their time of surprise;
for the woods are the first defence
and the first snare.

But on this day of heat
as I stand on the old rampart
the hill falls smooth away
to the plain below
shorn and parted and tilled;
and I see no woods advance,
nor any man at all
except, as it might be, you
standing there in the opening
where the great gate once stood.

With flint and fire and iron
they hewed and hacked at the trees
for stakes and gates and stockades;

for this ditch delved twice as deep,
this rampart twice as high
thrust up into a steep.
And the inner circle bristled
with thatch, prickled with the thin
sting of wood-smoke, where now
is the scent of warm turf only,
sweet as a cheek new-shorn.
And the call and clatter and bustle
of women and children and men,
and sheep and cattle and swine,
brimmed full this broad circle
where now the only sound
is lark-song hanging above,
and where you wander alone.

But I still stand on the rampart
looking out and in,
and marvel how under my feet
walls were once straight and steep
that are now a gentle slope,
smooth as the trees outside,
as the roof-trees within.
And my own defences too
will be worn away in time,
smoothed down by time and you.

A Wardian Case

The vanilla scent of damp chestnut leaves
golden in falling, soft brown underfoot,
spices the air
and I'm back there, in still another
of those childhood avenues that lead straight
as spokes to this place where I find myself.

The turnstile spins. Kew is all mine today.
Along which walk shall I wander? to re-possess
this gold and bronze, help the horse-carts
collect dead leaves, punch the soft bark
of unbruising sequoia, a child's amazement.
There are spring paths, and summer; daffodils,
magnolia, a wash of bluebells. But today,
black boughs veining an agate sky, I touch
autumn, and it embraces me back.

Memory, like a Wardian case, brings live
instants out of the past, encapsulated
each in its particular atmosphere.
The glass dome's ark sealed against time and weather
ferries time breathing still:
as botanists once brought round half the world
those stoppered rarities, whose alien bubbles
released their relish into the Palm House, mingling
a richness of air, an enclosed safety of marvels.
Today, the scent
of chestnut leaves gives me the Gardens back.
Spiced air and loss thicken my throat again.

The Camden Town Murders

Sickert in the barber's chair
bares his throat to the razor

a clean jaw the sign of
civilisation in a man

imagines the sting of parting skin
springing aside of elastic flesh

behind his eyelids always ready
the canvas primed and stretched

collarbone to cheekbone
honed line of the naked neck

bisected by the keen edge
eager as his brush

feels the blade hiss as it kisses
hears through his blood the sigh

of Emily's second, scarlet
mouth; puts himself in the picture.

Sickert cleanshaven
looks in the barber's mirror

as at a portrait
sees himself full-bearded

knows that the difference
between what is and is not

rests on a knife-edge.

Running with the Unicorns

For Irene, because of Mary

Those first years must have seemed
a sort of Eden by comparison
after her father, sword-sharp with the light
of his Damascus vision, pronounced the edict:
from now on, a life without worldly pleasures,
no colour, music, human affection, only
God.

        And she at five years old
put on her drab dresses, learned to walk modestly,
and not to run or skip. They could read the Bible,
sing hymns at worship. She endured the taunts
of her schoolfellows like a crown of thorns.
Her father played Little God, exacted
precise obedience; her mother bowed her head,
"Be it unto me according to thy word."

War released her to the factory: too late. She was ill at ease
with other girls, the bright inconsequent chatter
of clothes and men; knew lipstick was a sin,
dancing the devil's work, that bore fruit sometimes.
They jeered at her dull garments, her strict plaits,
her discomfort when they swore. She suffered everything
with patience, would not answer back
but held herself aloof. The world was dangerous,
the rules were known and safe.

Later, her parents dead, she worked alone
at orchard and gardens. Perfection was permitted,
the apple of sin redeemed by virtuous pruning.

What secret solace here! the scent of fruit,
the crisp unfolding lettuce, softness of blooms
beneath her roughened fingers. She worked her hands
deep in the sun-warmed earth, and felt contentment
rise like a breath of peace, but never thought
that this was worldly pleasure. Such was God's mercy.

When she died, the Brethren gathered like a flock
of scavenging birds. "In the arms of the Lord," they said.
What should she know
of the arms of Jesus, she who never since
that grim enforced conversion, felt even
her own mother's arms? Heaven must have frightened her,
insensible of love, innocent of the least shadow
of glory, terrified by the dissolution
of the known, prisoning body.

I pray she found herself
reborn to brightness with such incredulous joy
as some old weary horse set free at last
from harness-gall and knackers' yard, finding his shambles
of broken bones radiantly embodied, and he
amazed in clear heraldic colours, *argent
on a field vert*, running with the unicorns.